T0065276

MY OWN TRAVEL JOURNAL

THINGS I WANT TO REMEMBER

authorHOUSE®

AuthorHouse™
1663 Liberty Drive
Bloomington, IN 47403
www.authorhouse.com
Phone: 1 (800) 839-8640

Published by AuthorHouse 02/12/2016

ISBN: 978-1-5049-7597-1 (sc)
ISBN: 978-1-5049-7596-4 (e)

This book belongs to _____

This is your own travel journal. No one else gets to write in it. Travel journals have been used for decades, even centuries, to document the sights, sounds and experiences of travelers. Did you know that Christopher Columbus kept a travel journal? Just imagine what his journal looked like! The new sights he saw, the events and obstacles he encountered, even the feelings he had. You don't have to imagine. You can do a search and find a link to the journal of Christopher Columbus!

How to use this journal:

This journal has room for more than one trip. You could use the same journal for next year's vacation if you like. So keep it in a safe place.

For each trip you take, you'll start by filling out the information on the first page. List who you are traveling with, where you are headed and why you're going there. **Be sure to date every entry you make.**

Every day, write what you experienced. Examples:

- **Where** you went (what city, amusement park, national park)

- **Who** you saw (relatives, people from other countries, celebrities)

- **What** you saw (mountains, lakes, beaches, a museum, a zoo, animals, birds)

- **How** you felt (joyful, surprised, excited, nervous, etc.)

As you write in your journal, you may begin to notice more details around you. That's a good thing! You can draw pictures of what you saw – or on the days you stop at a gift shop, buy a post card from the place you're visiting. Except for the first page of the trip, the pages are mostly blank, so you can write, draw a picture or tape a post card on any page. Leave room for photos you take, and put them in later.

You can start your journal on any day of your trip, but once you start, try to do it every day. You can even write in a journal when you get home. Lots of people journal every day. On the next page are some ideas to help you get started.

Have a great trip!

How to begin:

Before you start writing, close your eyes, take a breath and remember what you saw today.

What did you notice? Then just start writing. You don't need to worry about making mistakes. This is YOUR journal. Just write!

Some ideas you might want to write about:

❖ What did the scenery look like? Mountains? Lakes? Corn fields? Anything really unusual?

❖ What was the weather like today?

❖ Did you notice animals or birds? What were they doing? How did they sound?

❖ Did you see or talk to people from other states or other countries?

❖ What did you do today? Did you hike, go swimming, ride a roller coaster, try a new food, go to a museum, sing in the car?

❖ Did you get any souvenirs today?

MY OWN TRAVEL JOURNAL

DATE WE STARTED: _____

REASON FOR THIS TRIP: _____

_____

_____

_____

WHO IS TRAVELING: _____

_____

_____

_____

VEHICLE WE'RE TRAVELING IN: _____

MY OWN TRAVEL JOURNAL

TODAY'S DATE _____

MY OBSERVATIONS, AND WHAT WAS THE BEST PART ABOUT
TODAY:

MY OWN TRAVEL JOURNAL

TODAY'S DATE _____

MY OBSERVATIONS, AND WHAT WAS THE BEST PART ABOUT TODAY:

MY OWN TRAVEL JOURNAL

TODAY'S DATE _____

MY OBSERVATIONS, AND WHAT WAS THE BEST PART ABOUT
TODAY:

MY OWN TRAVEL JOURNAL

TODAY'S DATE _____

MY OBSERVATIONS, AND WHAT WAS THE BEST PART ABOUT TODAY:

MY OWN TRAVEL JOURNAL

TODAY'S DATE _____

MY OBSERVATIONS, AND WHAT WAS THE BEST PART ABOUT TODAY:

MY OWN TRAVEL JOURNAL

TODAY'S DATE _____

MY OBSERVATIONS, AND WHAT WAS THE BEST PART ABOUT
TODAY:

MY OWN TRAVEL JOURNAL

TODAY'S DATE _____

MY OBSERVATIONS, AND WHAT WAS THE BEST PART ABOUT
TODAY:

MY OWN TRAVEL JOURNAL

TODAY'S DATE _____

MY OBSERVATIONS, AND WHAT WAS THE BEST PART ABOUT TODAY:

MY OWN TRAVEL JOURNAL

TODAY'S DATE _____

MY OBSERVATIONS, AND WHAT WAS THE BEST PART ABOUT
TODAY:

MY OWN TRAVEL JOURNAL

TODAY'S DATE _____

MY OBSERVATIONS, AND WHAT WAS THE BEST PART ABOUT
TODAY:

MY OWN TRAVEL JOURNAL

TODAY'S DATE _____

MY OBSERVATIONS, AND WHAT WAS THE BEST PART ABOUT TODAY:

MY OWN TRAVEL JOURNAL

TODAY'S DATE _____

MY OBSERVATIONS, AND WHAT WAS THE BEST PART ABOUT
TODAY:

MY OWN TRAVEL JOURNAL

TODAY'S DATE _____

MY OBSERVATIONS, AND WHAT WAS THE BEST PART ABOUT
TODAY:

MY OWN TRAVEL JOURNAL

TODAY'S DATE _____

MY OBSERVATIONS, AND WHAT WAS THE BEST PART ABOUT
TODAY:

MY OWN TRAVEL JOURNAL

TODAY'S DATE _____

MY OBSERVATIONS, AND WHAT WAS THE BEST PART ABOUT
TODAY:

MY OWN TRAVEL JOURNAL

TODAY'S DATE _____

MY OBSERVATIONS, AND WHAT WAS THE BEST PART ABOUT
TODAY:

MY OWN TRAVEL JOURNAL

TODAY'S DATE _____

MY OBSERVATIONS, AND WHAT WAS THE BEST PART ABOUT
TODAY:

MY OWN TRAVEL JOURNAL

TODAY'S DATE _____

MY OBSERVATIONS, AND WHAT WAS THE BEST PART ABOUT
TODAY:

MY OWN TRAVEL JOURNAL

TODAY'S DATE _____

MY OBSERVATIONS, AND WHAT WAS THE BEST PART ABOUT
TODAY:

MY OWN TRAVEL JOURNAL

TODAY'S DATE _____

MY OBSERVATIONS, AND WHAT WAS THE BEST PART ABOUT
TODAY:

MY OWN TRAVEL JOURNAL

TODAY'S DATE _____

MY OBSERVATIONS, AND WHAT WAS THE BEST PART ABOUT
TODAY:

MY OWN TRAVEL JOURNAL

TODAY'S DATE _____

MY OBSERVATIONS, AND WHAT WAS THE BEST PART ABOUT
TODAY:

MY OWN TRAVEL JOURNAL

TODAY'S DATE _____

MY OBSERVATIONS, AND WHAT WAS THE BEST PART ABOUT
TODAY:

MY OWN TRAVEL JOURNAL

TODAY'S DATE _____

MY OBSERVATIONS, AND WHAT WAS THE BEST PART ABOUT
TODAY:

MY OWN TRAVEL JOURNAL

TODAY'S DATE _____

MY OBSERVATIONS, AND WHAT WAS THE BEST PART ABOUT
TODAY:

MY OWN TRAVEL JOURNAL

TODAY'S DATE _____

MY OBSERVATIONS, AND WHAT WAS THE BEST PART ABOUT TODAY:

MY OWN TRAVEL JOURNAL

TODAY'S DATE _____

MY OBSERVATIONS, AND WHAT WAS THE BEST PART ABOUT
TODAY:

MY OWN TRAVEL JOURNAL

TODAY'S DATE _____

MY OBSERVATIONS, AND WHAT WAS THE BEST PART ABOUT
TODAY:

MY OWN TRAVEL JOURNAL

TODAY'S DATE _____

MY OBSERVATIONS, AND WHAT WAS THE BEST PART ABOUT
TODAY:

MY OWN TRAVEL JOURNAL

TODAY'S DATE _____

MY OBSERVATIONS, AND WHAT WAS THE BEST PART ABOUT
TODAY:

MY OWN TRAVEL JOURNAL

TODAY'S DATE _____

MY OBSERVATIONS, AND WHAT WAS THE BEST PART ABOUT
TODAY:

MY OWN TRAVEL JOURNAL

TODAY'S DATE _____

MY OBSERVATIONS, AND WHAT WAS THE BEST PART ABOUT
TODAY:

MY OWN TRAVEL JOURNAL

TODAY'S DATE _____

MY OBSERVATIONS, AND WHAT WAS THE BEST PART ABOUT
TODAY:

MY OWN TRAVEL JOURNAL

TODAY'S DATE _____

MY OBSERVATIONS, AND WHAT WAS THE BEST PART ABOUT
TODAY:

MY OWN TRAVEL JOURNAL

TODAY'S DATE _____

MY OBSERVATIONS, AND WHAT WAS THE BEST PART ABOUT
TODAY:

MY OWN TRAVEL JOURNAL

TODAY'S DATE _____

MY OBSERVATIONS, AND WHAT WAS THE BEST PART ABOUT
TODAY:

MY OWN TRAVEL JOURNAL

TODAY'S DATE _____

MY OBSERVATIONS, AND WHAT WAS THE BEST PART ABOUT
TODAY:

MY OWN TRAVEL JOURNAL

TODAY'S DATE _____

MY OBSERVATIONS, AND WHAT WAS THE BEST PART ABOUT
TODAY:

MY OWN TRAVEL JOURNAL

TODAY'S DATE _____

MY OBSERVATIONS, AND WHAT WAS THE BEST PART ABOUT
TODAY:

MY OWN TRAVEL JOURNAL

TODAY'S DATE _____

MY OBSERVATIONS, AND WHAT WAS THE BEST PART ABOUT
TODAY:

MY OWN TRAVEL JOURNAL

TODAY'S DATE _____

MY OBSERVATIONS, AND WHAT WAS THE BEST PART ABOUT
TODAY:

MY OWN TRAVEL JOURNAL

TODAY'S DATE _____

MY OBSERVATIONS, AND WHAT WAS THE BEST PART ABOUT TODAY:

MY OWN TRAVEL JOURNAL

TODAY'S DATE _____

MY OBSERVATIONS, AND WHAT WAS THE BEST PART ABOUT
TODAY:

MY OWN TRAVEL JOURNAL

TODAY'S DATE _____

MY OBSERVATIONS, AND WHAT WAS THE BEST PART ABOUT
TODAY:

MY OWN TRAVEL JOURNAL

TODAY'S DATE _____

MY OBSERVATIONS, AND WHAT WAS THE BEST PART ABOUT
TODAY:

MY OWN TRAVEL JOURNAL

TODAY'S DATE _____

MY OBSERVATIONS, AND WHAT WAS THE BEST PART ABOUT
TODAY:

MY OWN TRAVEL JOURNAL

DATE WE STARTED: _____

REASON FOR THIS TRIP: _____

_____

_____

_____

WHO IS TRAVELING: _____

_____

_____

_____

VEHICLE WE'RE TRAVELING IN: _____

MY OWN TRAVEL JOURNAL

TODAY'S DATE _____

MY OBSERVATIONS, AND WHAT WAS THE BEST PART ABOUT
TODAY:

MY OWN TRAVEL JOURNAL

TODAY'S DATE _____

MY OBSERVATIONS, AND WHAT WAS THE BEST PART ABOUT
TODAY:

MY OWN TRAVEL JOURNAL

TODAY'S DATE _____

MY OBSERVATIONS, AND WHAT WAS THE BEST PART ABOUT
TODAY:

MY OWN TRAVEL JOURNAL

TODAY'S DATE _____

MY OBSERVATIONS, AND WHAT WAS THE BEST PART ABOUT
TODAY:

MY OWN TRAVEL JOURNAL

TODAY'S DATE _____

MY OBSERVATIONS, AND WHAT WAS THE BEST PART ABOUT
TODAY:

MY OWN TRAVEL JOURNAL

TODAY'S DATE _____

MY OBSERVATIONS, AND WHAT WAS THE BEST PART ABOUT TODAY:

MY OWN TRAVEL JOURNAL

TODAY'S DATE _____

MY OBSERVATIONS, AND WHAT WAS THE BEST PART ABOUT
TODAY:

MY OWN TRAVEL JOURNAL

TODAY'S DATE _____

MY OBSERVATIONS, AND WHAT WAS THE BEST PART ABOUT
TODAY:

MY OWN TRAVEL JOURNAL

TODAY'S DATE _____

MY OBSERVATIONS, AND WHAT WAS THE BEST PART ABOUT
TODAY:

MY OWN TRAVEL JOURNAL

TODAY'S DATE _____

MY OBSERVATIONS, AND WHAT WAS THE BEST PART ABOUT
TODAY:

MY OWN TRAVEL JOURNAL

TODAY'S DATE _____

MY OBSERVATIONS, AND WHAT WAS THE BEST PART ABOUT
TODAY:

MY OWN TRAVEL JOURNAL

TODAY'S DATE _____

MY OBSERVATIONS, AND WHAT WAS THE BEST PART ABOUT
TODAY:

MY OWN TRAVEL JOURNAL

TODAY'S DATE _____

MY OBSERVATIONS, AND WHAT WAS THE BEST PART ABOUT
TODAY:

MY OWN TRAVEL JOURNAL

TODAY'S DATE _____

MY OBSERVATIONS, AND WHAT WAS THE BEST PART ABOUT
TODAY:

MY OWN TRAVEL JOURNAL

TODAY'S DATE _____

MY OBSERVATIONS, AND WHAT WAS THE BEST PART ABOUT
TODAY:

MY OWN TRAVEL JOURNAL

TODAY'S DATE _____

MY OBSERVATIONS, AND WHAT WAS THE BEST PART ABOUT
TODAY:

MY OWN TRAVEL JOURNAL

TODAY'S DATE _____

MY OBSERVATIONS, AND WHAT WAS THE BEST PART ABOUT
TODAY:

MY OWN TRAVEL JOURNAL

TODAY'S DATE _____

MY OBSERVATIONS, AND WHAT WAS THE BEST PART ABOUT
TODAY:

MY OWN TRAVEL JOURNAL

TODAY'S DATE _____

MY OBSERVATIONS, AND WHAT WAS THE BEST PART ABOUT
TODAY:

MY OWN TRAVEL JOURNAL

TODAY'S DATE _____

MY OBSERVATIONS, AND WHAT WAS THE BEST PART ABOUT
TODAY:

MY OWN TRAVEL JOURNAL

TODAY'S DATE _____

MY OBSERVATIONS, AND WHAT WAS THE BEST PART ABOUT
TODAY:

MY OWN TRAVEL JOURNAL

TODAY'S DATE _____

MY OBSERVATIONS, AND WHAT WAS THE BEST PART ABOUT
TODAY:

MY OWN TRAVEL JOURNAL

TODAY'S DATE _____

MY OBSERVATIONS, AND WHAT WAS THE BEST PART ABOUT
TODAY:

MY OWN TRAVEL JOURNAL

TODAY'S DATE _____

MY OBSERVATIONS, AND WHAT WAS THE BEST PART ABOUT
TODAY:

MY OWN TRAVEL JOURNAL

TODAY'S DATE _____

MY OBSERVATIONS, AND WHAT WAS THE BEST PART ABOUT
TODAY:

MY OWN TRAVEL JOURNAL

TODAY'S DATE _____

MY OBSERVATIONS, AND WHAT WAS THE BEST PART ABOUT
TODAY:

MY OWN TRAVEL JOURNAL

TODAY'S DATE _____

MY OBSERVATIONS, AND WHAT WAS THE BEST PART ABOUT
TODAY:

MY OWN TRAVEL JOURNAL

TODAY'S DATE _____

MY OBSERVATIONS, AND WHAT WAS THE BEST PART ABOUT
TODAY:

MY OWN TRAVEL JOURNAL

TODAY'S DATE _____

MY OBSERVATIONS, AND WHAT WAS THE BEST PART ABOUT
TODAY:

MY OWN TRAVEL JOURNAL

TODAY'S DATE _____

MY OBSERVATIONS, AND WHAT WAS THE BEST PART ABOUT
TODAY:

MY OWN TRAVEL JOURNAL

TODAY'S DATE _____

MY OBSERVATIONS, AND WHAT WAS THE BEST PART ABOUT
TODAY:

MY OWN TRAVEL JOURNAL

TODAY'S DATE _____

MY OBSERVATIONS, AND WHAT WAS THE BEST PART ABOUT
TODAY:

MY OWN TRAVEL JOURNAL

TODAY'S DATE _____

MY OBSERVATIONS, AND WHAT WAS THE BEST PART ABOUT
TODAY:

MY OWN TRAVEL JOURNAL

TODAY'S DATE _____

MY OBSERVATIONS, AND WHAT WAS THE BEST PART ABOUT
TODAY:

MY OWN TRAVEL JOURNAL

TODAY'S DATE _____

MY OBSERVATIONS, AND WHAT WAS THE BEST PART ABOUT
TODAY:

MY OWN TRAVEL JOURNAL

TODAY'S DATE _____

MY OBSERVATIONS, AND WHAT WAS THE BEST PART ABOUT
TODAY:

MY OWN TRAVEL JOURNAL

TODAY'S DATE _____

MY OBSERVATIONS, AND WHAT WAS THE BEST PART ABOUT
TODAY:

MY OWN TRAVEL JOURNAL

TODAY'S DATE _____

MY OBSERVATIONS, AND WHAT WAS THE BEST PART ABOUT
TODAY:

MY OWN TRAVEL JOURNAL

TODAY'S DATE _____

MY OBSERVATIONS, AND WHAT WAS THE BEST PART ABOUT
TODAY:

MY OWN TRAVEL JOURNAL

TODAY'S DATE _____

MY OBSERVATIONS, AND WHAT WAS THE BEST PART ABOUT
TODAY:

MY OWN TRAVEL JOURNAL

TODAY'S DATE _____

MY OBSERVATIONS, AND WHAT WAS THE BEST PART ABOUT
TODAY:

MY OWN TRAVEL JOURNAL

TODAY'S DATE _____

MY OBSERVATIONS, AND WHAT WAS THE BEST PART ABOUT
TODAY:

MY OWN TRAVEL JOURNAL

TODAY'S DATE _____

MY OBSERVATIONS, AND WHAT WAS THE BEST PART ABOUT
TODAY:

Printed in the United States
By Bookmasters